Forecasting Disasters

TORNADOES

Dalton Rains

Copyright © 2026 by Apex Editions, Mendota Heights, MN 55120. All rights reserved. No part of this book may be reproduced or utilized in any form or by any means without written permission from the publisher.

Apex is distributed by North Star Editions:
sales@northstareditions.com | 888-417-0195

Produced for Apex by Red Line Editorial.

Photographs ©: Shutterstock Images, cover, 1, 4–5, 10–11, 12–13, 14–15, 16–17, 26–27, 28–29, 30–31, 32–33, 36–37, 39, 44–45, 50–51, 52–53, 54–55, 58; Sandra J. Milburn/The Hutchinson News/AP Images, 6–7; Scott Olson/Getty Images News/Getty Images, 8–9; Joe Raedle/Getty Images News/Getty Images, 18–19; Library of Congress, 20–21; Tinker Air Force Base History Office/NOAA, 22–23; AP Images, 24–25; NEXRAD, 34–35; Michael Smith/The Wyoming Tribune Eagle/AP Images, 40–41; NOAA/Getty Images News/Getty Images, 42–43; Adam Robison/The Northeast Mississippi Daily Journal/AP Images, 46–47; Heather Ainsworth/AP Images, 49; Drew Angerer/Getty Images News/Getty Images, 56–57

Library of Congress Control Number: 2025930909

ISBN
979-8-89250-663-2 (hardcover)
979-8-89250-698-4 (ebook pdf)
979-8-89250-681-6 (hosted ebook)

Printed in the United States of America
Mankato, MN
082025

NOTE TO PARENTS AND EDUCATORS

Apex books are designed to build literacy skills in striving readers. Exciting, high-interest content attracts and holds readers' attention. The text is carefully leveled to allow students to achieve success quickly.

TABLE OF CONTENTS

Chapter 1
DEADLY STORM 4

Chapter 2
ALL ABOUT TORNADOES 10

Chapter 3
EARLY HISTORY 20

Chapter 4
TORNADO TROUBLES 29

That's Wild!
RADAR TO THE RESCUE 38

Chapter 5
COMPLEX CALCULATIONS 41

That's Wild!
TORNADO TEXTS 48

Chapter 6
FUTURE FORECASTING 50

TIMELINE • 59
COMPREHENSION QUESTIONS • 60
GLOSSARY • 62
TO LEARN MORE • 63
ABOUT THE AUTHOR • 63
INDEX • 64

Chapter 1
DEADLY STORM

Storm clouds roll over a family's home. They live in Dawson Springs, Kentucky. Soon, the National Weather Service (NWS) issues a tornado warning. The NWS posts the warning on social media. Tornado sirens blare. The family takes cover.

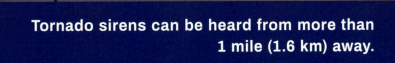

Tornado sirens can be heard from more than 1 mile (1.6 km) away.

Thunder rumbles outside. Suddenly, a tornado slams into the family's house. Wind blasts through the walls. It reaches speeds of 190 miles per hour (305 km/h). The house's windows shatter. Wooden beams snap.

STAYING SAFE

During a tornado, the basement is usually the safest part of a home. If there is no basement, people should find a spot with no windows. This may be a hallway. It may be a closet or bathroom.

Tornadoes kick up dirt and debris as they pass over land.

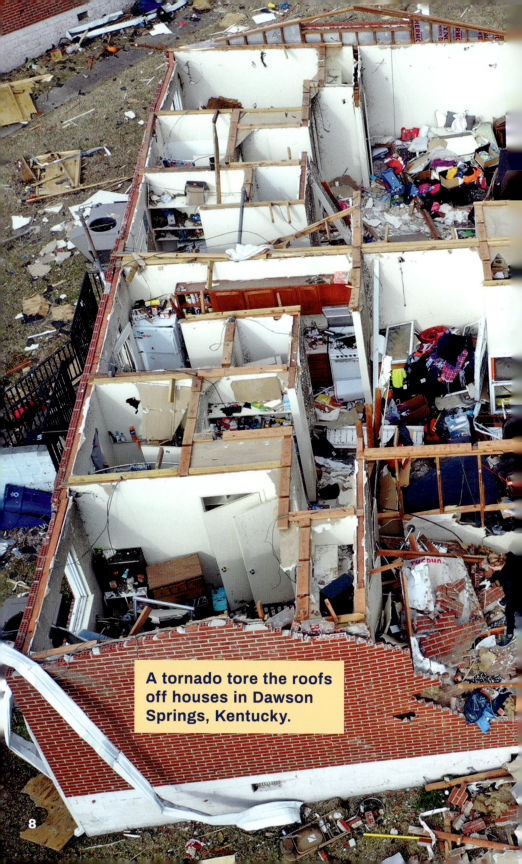

A tornado tore the roofs off houses in Dawson Springs, Kentucky.

8

Within seconds, the tornado passes. Most of the house is destroyed. Outside, the tornado has toppled fences and power lines. It has even uprooted trees. But the family is safe. The early warning saved their lives.

LOST LIVES

On December 10, 2021, tornadoes struck parts of Kentucky and Tennessee. People received warnings. But the tornadoes caused heavy damage. Fifteen people died in Dawson Springs, Kentucky. In total, the tornadoes killed 57 people. Hundreds more were hurt.

Chapter 2

ALL ABOUT TORNADOES

Tornadoes are columns of spinning air. A tornado's winds can reach speeds of more than 300 miles per hour (480 km/h). Tornadoes usually happen in huge, swirling storms. These storms are called supercells.

Most tornadoes happen in the late afternoon or early evening.

For a tornado to form, a storm must have upward-moving air. The air must be able to rise very high. The storm must also have lots of moisture. Finally, the storm's winds must move in different directions at different heights. That causes some parts of the storm to rotate.

SPINNING STORMS

Inside supercells, warm air rises quickly in a spinning column. The air cools and forms clouds as it gets higher. Then, the cooled air and clouds sink back down. And more warm air moves up through the spinning column.

Moisture is one of the main things that gives a storm energy.

About 500 tornadoes happen in Tornado Alley every year.

Tornadoes can strike almost anywhere. They happen on every continent except Antarctica. However, the United States has more tornadoes than any other country. Each year, more than 1,000 tornadoes happen there.

TORNADO ALLEY

Tornado Alley covers the middle part of the United States. Many of the world's largest tornadoes happen in this region. Dry, cold air comes down from Canada. That air mixes with moist, warm air from the Gulf of Mexico.

15

Tornadoes are strong enough to bend metal around poles.

A tornado can cause massive damage. It may throw cars into the air. It may destroy buildings. Often, a tornado's high-speed winds pick up loose objects. The objects turn into deadly shrapnel. This flying debris is usually the biggest danger to people.

Scientists use a scale to measure the strength of tornadoes. It is called the EF Scale. The scale goes from EF0 to EF5. An EF0 tornado is the weakest. It has winds of 65 to 85 miles per hour (105 to 137 km/h). An EF5 tornado is the strongest. It has winds of more than 200 miles per hour (322 km/h).

JOPLIN

In 2011, an EF5 tornado ripped through Joplin, Missouri. The tornado destroyed thousands of buildings. It killed 161 people. More than 1,000 others were hurt. It was the deadliest single tornado in US history.

Survivors look at the destruction after the Joplin tornado.

Chapter 3

EARLY HISTORY

Tornado science goes back to the late 1800s. John Finley began some of the first research in 1882. He studied the weather conditions that led to tornadoes. However, tornado research did not become widespread until years later.

John Finley wrote a book on tornadoes and collected large amounts of weather data.

In 1948, a tornado tore through Tinker Air Force Base. This base is in Oklahoma. The tornado destroyed 117 aircraft. After that, people on the base studied tornadoes. Like Finley, they researched weather patterns. Some patterns tended to form tornadoes.

A plane lies in ruins after the 1948 tornado at Tinker Air Force Base.

FIRST FORECAST

The first official tornado forecast in the United States happened at Tinker Air Force Base. Scientists on the base said a tornado could happen on March 25, 1948. That night, a tornado formed. Thanks to the warning, no one was killed.

People wanted better forecasts. In 1952, the United States Weather Bureau took action. The bureau formed a Severe Local Storms (SELS) unit. Many tornadoes happened in 1953. SELS predict some of them. But it missed a few big ones. Scientists knew they had to do more research.

BIG MISSES

In 1953, SELS predicted a tornado in the southern United States. But scientists didn't realize it would hit Vicksburg, Mississippi. A huge tornado wiped out the town. SELS missed several other tornadoes that year. More than 300 people died. Many others were injured.

Workers clean up after a 1953 tornado in Waco, Texas.

During a tornado warning, people should find a safe place to take shelter.

In 1956, a tornado hit Indiana. It killed 266 people. SELS had predicted it. But many people didn't know about the forecast. So, SELS made warnings easier to understand. One type of warning is a tornado watch. It means a tornado is possible. Another type is a tornado warning. It means a tornado has been spotted or is expected soon.

TORNADO EMERGENCIES

A tornado emergency is the highest level of warning. These alerts are rare. They are sent only when large tornadoes are spotted on the ground.

Scientists who study the weather are called meteorologists.

Chapter 4
TORNADO TROUBLES

Weather science improved over the years. Scientists got better at recognizing weather patterns. They learned which conditions formed tornadoes. But it was still hard to know exactly which storms would form tornadoes.

Small tornadoes may last for a few minutes. Large tornadoes can last for more than an hour.

30

Compared to large storms such as hurricanes, tornadoes are small. That makes tornadoes hard to spot. Also, tornadoes start quickly. And they last only a few minutes. So, it's difficult to issue a warning more than a few minutes in advance.

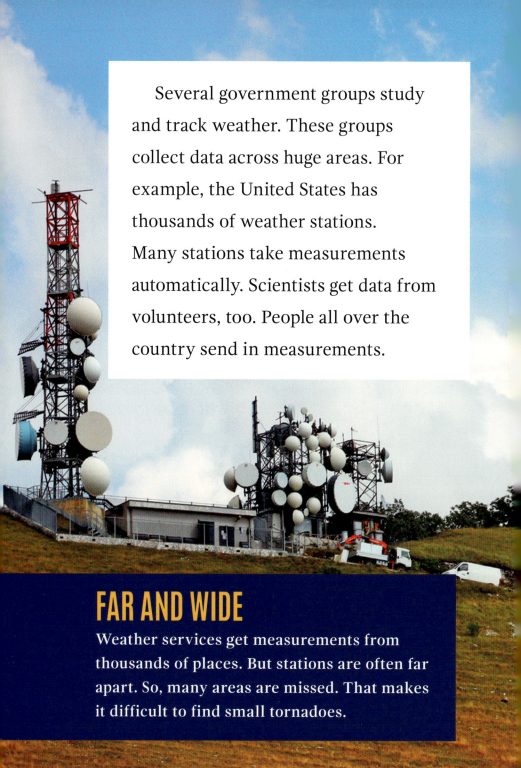

Several government groups study and track weather. These groups collect data across huge areas. For example, the United States has thousands of weather stations. Many stations take measurements automatically. Scientists get data from volunteers, too. People all over the country send in measurements.

FAR AND WIDE

Weather services get measurements from thousands of places. But stations are often far apart. So, many areas are missed. That makes it difficult to find small tornadoes.

Weather stations measure wind speeds, temperature, and humidity.

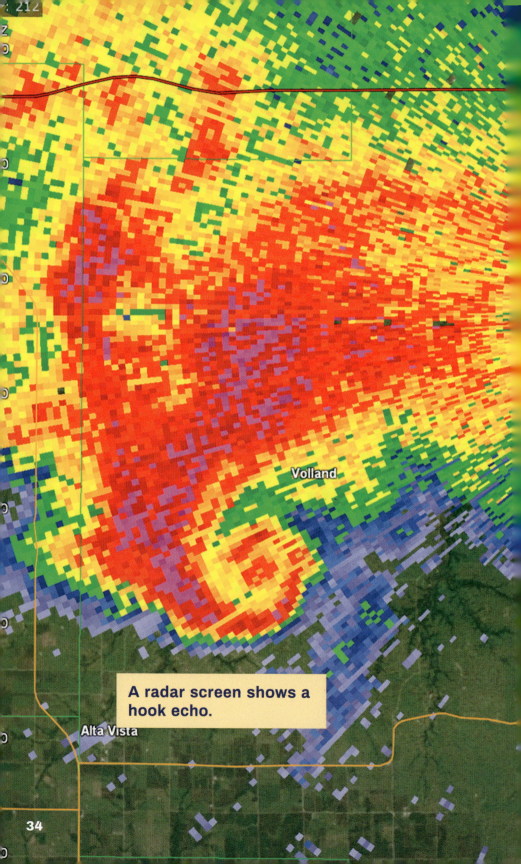

A radar screen shows a hook echo.

34

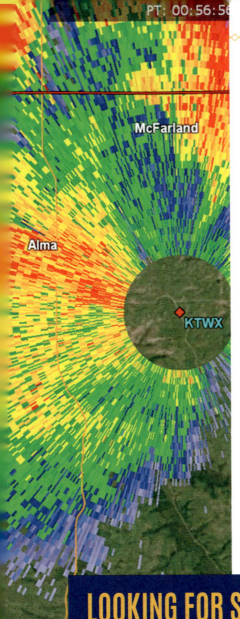

Doppler radar helps fill in more data. Doppler was first used to spot a tornado in 1973. By the 1990s, scientists had finished building a network. It included more than 100 Doppler radar sensors. The network helped scientists create detailed maps. The maps showed precipitation and wind.

LOOKING FOR SIGNS

Scientists study radar maps. They look for signs of tornadoes. Hook echoes are one type of pattern. They look like hook-shaped arms. Hook echoes stretch out from supercells. Other patterns show when debris is lifted high into the air.

Radar maps are helpful. But they don't show everything. Signs of tornadoes can be hard to spot. Sometimes radar doesn't pick up tornadoes at all. So, scientists may have to rely on other tools. Storm spotters on the ground often help.

Spotting storms can be a highly dangerous job.

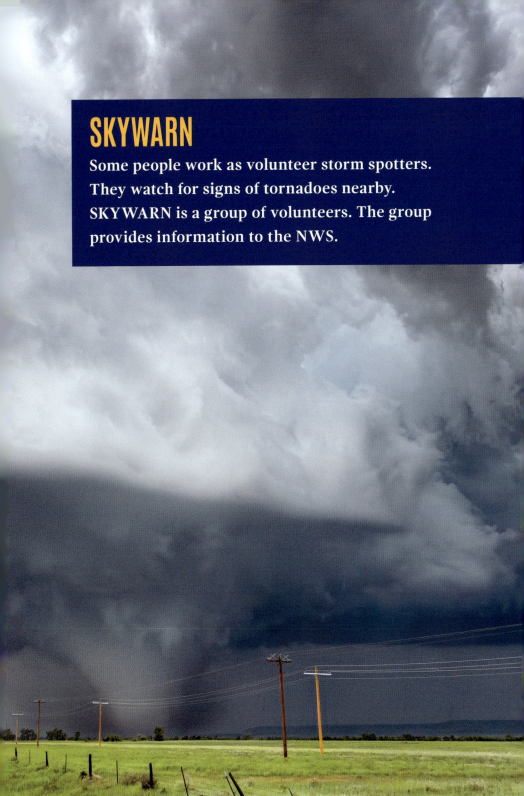

SKYWARN

Some people work as volunteer storm spotters. They watch for signs of tornadoes nearby. SKYWARN is a group of volunteers. The group provides information to the NWS.

That's Wild!
RADAR TO THE RESCUE

In 1982, two scientists were working at an NWS control room. It was in Norman, Oklahoma. The scientists studied a Doppler radar map. They noticed that nearby clouds had formed a spiral pattern. A tornado was about to form.

The scientists called another scientist in Oklahoma City. He sent out a warning. It was the first warning based on Doppler radar. The scientists warned people about 30 minutes before the tornado hit. They helped save lives.

A Doppler tower has a ball at the top to protect the antenna.

Scientists rely on massive supercomputers to do complicated weather calculations.

COMPLEX CALCULATIONS

Scientists create complicated math formulas. They add weather data to the formulas. Then, computers do the calculations. The formulas help predict how weather will play out.

To get accurate predictions, weather scientists need lots of measurements. They must also understand weather patterns. They add many variables to their formulas. Processing the data takes lots of computing power. The NWS uses supercomputers.

BIG DATA

Some weather patterns are small. Others cover huge areas. El Niño and La Niña are two large-scale patterns. These patterns have to do with the temperature of the Pacific Ocean. Scientists study other large-scale patterns, too. Some have to do with rainfall or cloud cover.

Computers can help scientists study cloud patterns that may lead to tornadoes.

Armored vehicles help people stay safer when they chase storms.

Long-range measurements sometimes aren't enough for computer models. So, storm chasers help with up-close measurements. They use close-range radar. These sensors give scientists a better view of a tornado. Other sensors measure humidity or air pressure. Some storm chasers even use rockets. They send probes into tornadoes.

ARMOR AND ANCHORS

Storm chasers use heavy-duty trucks. Steel armor blocks hail and debris. Thick windows do, too. The trucks may also have spikes. They can hold trucks to the ground. That keeps the trucks stable when winds are strong.

During tornadoes, TV stations can let people know that they need to get to safety.

Computer models help scientists send out faster warnings. NWS warnings usually happen 10 to 15 minutes before a tornado strikes. To get the word out, officials use local news and weather radio. They also use social media. Many places have tornado sirens, too.

WAYS TO WARN

Scientists often use TV to send out important information. Tornado warnings may interrupt shows on TV. Banners may stay on the bottom of the screen. That way, people can keep getting updates.

That's Wild!

TORNADO TEXTS

Scientists continue to find new ways to send tornado warnings. Sometimes, they use text messages. They send warnings straight to people's phones. These are called Wireless Emergency Alerts (WEAs).

In 2012, a strong tornado struck Elmira, New York. It completely destroyed four homes. Fallen trees damaged other buildings. However, there were no major injuries. Many people saw WEAs on their phones. They found shelter before the tornado hit.

> Since they first started in 2012, Wireless Emergency Alerts have saved many lives.

Chapter 6

FUTURE FORECASTING

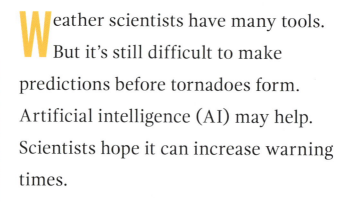

Weather scientists have many tools. But it's still difficult to make predictions before tornadoes form. Artificial intelligence (AI) may help. Scientists hope it can increase warning times.

Artificial intelligence can analyze weather conditions to help scientists make better predictions.

AI programs work like other computer models. Both need lots of data. Scientists put in measurements from past storms. AI programs go through the data. The programs figure out what led to tornadoes in the past. Then, scientists put in current data. The AI programs compare current patterns to past storms.

AI may help people get to safety before tornadoes strike.

53

Scientists think climate change may be causing more tornadoes in the southeastern United States.

Faster computers can help, too. Weather conditions are always changing. And scientists continue to learn about new patterns. So, there is more and more data to process. Scientists need powerful computers to handle it all.

CLIMATE CHANGE

Climate change is affecting weather patterns all over the world. But scientists are not sure how much it affects tornadoes. In some places, climate change may be causing more tornadoes. It may also be causing stronger tornadoes. However, more study is needed.

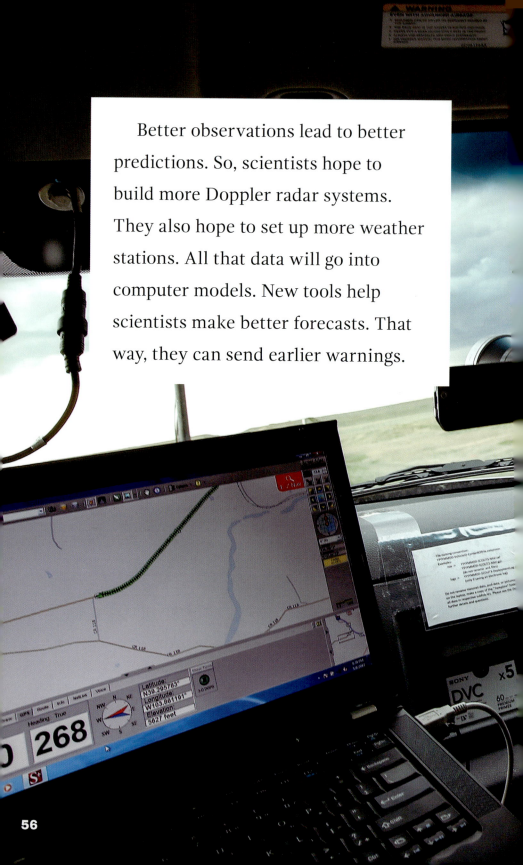

Better observations lead to better predictions. So, scientists hope to build more Doppler radar systems. They also hope to set up more weather stations. All that data will go into computer models. New tools help scientists make better forecasts. That way, they can send earlier warnings.

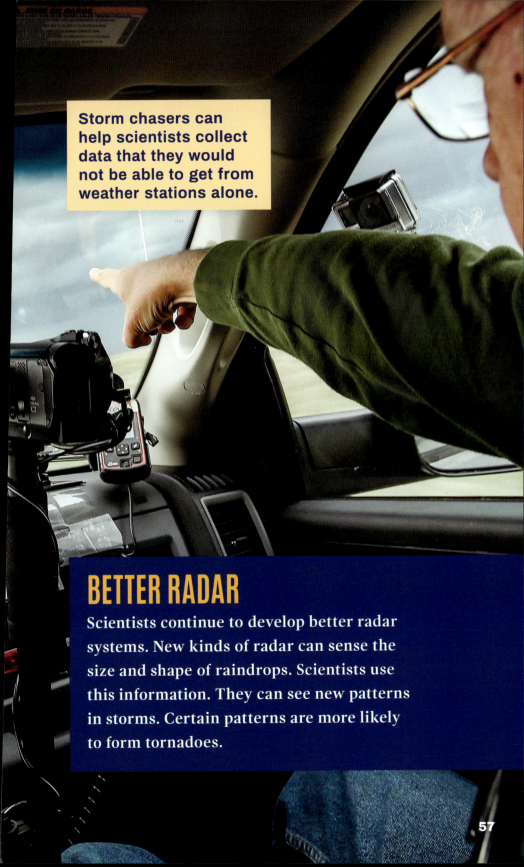

Storm chasers can help scientists collect data that they would not be able to get from weather stations alone.

BETTER RADAR

Scientists continue to develop better radar systems. New kinds of radar can sense the size and shape of raindrops. Scientists use this information. They can see new patterns in storms. Certain patterns are more likely to form tornadoes.

TIMELINE

1882 — John Finley performs some of the first tornado research.

1948 — The first official tornado forecast in the United States is issued on the evening of March 25 at Tinker Air Force Base in Oklahoma.

1952 — The United States Weather Bureau forms a Severe Local Storms (SELS) unit.

1956 — SELS starts a new system of tornado warnings that are easier to understand.

1973 — Scientists use Doppler radar to identify a tornado for the first time.

1982 — Oklahoma officials issue the first tornado warning based on Doppler radar.

2011 — An EF5 tornado rips through Joplin, Missouri, on May 22.

2021 — On December 10, several tornadoes strike Kentucky, Tennessee, and other nearby states.

COMPREHENSION QUESTIONS

Write your answers on a separate piece of paper.

1. Write a paragraph that explains the main ideas of Chapter 2.

2. Which kind of tornado warning do you think is most important? Why?

3. In what year did an EF5 tornado hit Joplin, Missouri?
   - A. 1982
   - B. 2011
   - C. 2012

4. How many years passed between the first time scientists spotted a tornado on Doppler radar and the first time scientists issued a warning based on Doppler radar?
   - A. two years
   - B. four years
   - C. nine years

5. What does **region** mean in this book?

   *Tornado Alley covers the middle part of the United States. Many of the world's largest tornadoes happen in this **region**.*

   A. height
   B. storm
   C. area

6. What does **develop** mean in this book?

   *Scientists continue to **develop** better radar systems. New kinds of radar can sense the size and shape of raindrops.*

   A. work on breaking something
   B. work on making something
   C. work on ending something

Answer key on page 64.

GLOSSARY

artificial intelligence
Computer systems that can learn and change without following new instructions.

data
Information collected to study or track something.

debris
Pieces of something that broke or fell apart.

network
A large group of things that are connected together.

precipitation
Water that falls to the ground as rain, sleet, hail, or snow.

predict
To say what will happen in the future.

probes
Unmanned devices that take measurements.

radar
A system that uses radio waves to find the position or speed of something.

shrapnel
Broken pieces that move very quickly.

variables
Factors that can change or affect something.

volunteers
People who help without being paid.

TO LEARN MORE

BOOKS

Rains, Dalton. *Storm Chasers*. Apex Editions, 2025.

Rossiter, Brienna. *Tornadoes*. Apex Editions, 2023.

Sommer, Nathan. *The Joplin Tornado*. Bellwether Media, 2022.

ONLINE RESOURCES

Visit **www.apexeditions.com** to find links and resources related to this title.

ABOUT THE AUTHOR

Dalton Rains is an author and editor from Saint Paul, Minnesota.

INDEX

air pressure, 45
armored trucks, 45
artificial intelligence, 50, 52

climate change, 55
computer models, 45, 47, 52, 56

Dawson Springs, Kentucky, 5, 9
Doppler radar, 35, 38, 56

EF Scale, 18
Elmira, New York, 48
El Niño, 42

Finley, John, 20, 22

hook echoes, 35

Joplin, Missouri, 18

La Niña, 42

maps, 35–36, 38
measurements, 18, 32, 42, 45, 52

moisture, 12, 15

National Weather Service (NWS), 5, 37, 38, 42, 47

probes, 45

Severe Local Storms (SELS) unit, 24, 27
sirens, 5, 47
SKYWARN, 37
social media, 5, 47
storm spotters, 36–37, 45
supercomputers, 42, 55

text messages, 48
Tinker Air Force Base, 22–23
Tornado Alley, 15

Vicksburg, Mississippi, 24

weather stations, 32, 56
wind speeds, 6, 10, 18
Wireless Emergency Alerts (WEAs), 48

ANSWER KEY:

1. Answers will vary; 2. Answers will vary; 3. B; 4. C; 5. C; 6. B